I am...

dedicated to myself
for I am determined, inspired and strong.

written by J L Smith

illustrated by Alex Miles

An affirmation is a positive statement that confirms what is true about oneself. It is emotional support and encouragement that helps someone to believe in their potential. It transforms a person's thinking and inspires them. If someone can transform their thinking, they can transform their reality and their life.

In the back of the book you will find questions, exercises and challenges designed for you to do with your child(ren) or student(s) in order to explain what affirmations are and give some easy ways to use them. You will also find a glossary with easy to understand, age appropriate definitions of the words used throughout the book.

I am accomplished, appreciated and amazing.

I am beautiful, bold and brave.

Cc

I am caring, confident and courageous.

I am daring, determined and devoted.

Ee

I am enthusiastic and encouraging.

Ff

I am funny, friendly and fabulous.

I am guided, grateful and generous.

I am helpful, happy and humble.

Ii

I am intelligent, inspired and important.

I am joyful and jubilant.

Kk

I am kind and keen.

L l

I am loved, loving and loyal.

Mm

I am motivated and marvelous.

Nn

I am needed, nurturing and nice.

I am outgoing, observant and optimistic.

I am powerful, passionate and patriotic.

I am quick, quirky and qualified.

I am responsible, respected and remarkable.

Ss

I am successful and strong.

I am talented, tenacious and truthful.

Uu

I am unique and useful.

I am vibrant and valuable.

Ww

I am wacky, wild and whimsical.

I am experienced, extraordinary and excellent.

I am youthful and yearning.

I am zestful and zany.

Glossary

Accomplished: has been able to do many things and has done them well

Appreciated: people are thankful for what you do and are glad to have you around

Amazing: great, awesome

Beautiful: very pretty

Bold: someone who stands out

Brave: not afraid to do anything

Caring: takes care of others, cares about others

Confident: knows they can do it

Courageous: does something even if they are afraid

Daring: takes risks, tries new things

Determined: will finish no matter what

Devoted: will never give up

Enthusiastic: excited and ready to go

Encouraging: helps to show others the way

Funny: makes people laugh

Friendly: likes to talk to other people

Fabulous: makes people say "wow"

Guided: is shown the way or helped by others

Grateful: thankful

Generous: very giving

Helpful: makes things easier for other people, someone who helps

Happy: smiling and feeling good inside, in a good mood

Humble: happy to help without needing someone to say thank you

Intelligent: very smart

Inspired: feel like you should do something

Important: means a lot to others, is needed

Joyful: very happy, excited

Jubilant: feeling or showing great happiness

Kind: does nice things for people

Keen: very aware

Loved: gets love from someone

Loving: feels love for someone

Loyal: will always be there when others need them

Motivated: wants something very much and will work hard to get it

Marvelous: terrific, fantastic

Needed: others depend on you for help

Nurturing: likes to take care of others and help them get better or be better

Nice: not mean

Outgoing: likes to meet people and make friends

Observant: sees all that is going on, pays attention

Optimistic: believes that things will go well, is positive

Powerful: has control over people and things

Passionate: feels strongly about something

Patriotic: loves their country

Quick: fast

Quirky: different in a silly or strange way

Qualified: is able to do something well

Responsible: makes good choices

Respected: others look up to them

Remarkable: is worth noticing

Successful: able to finish something they say they will do

Strong: able to do difficult things

Talented: is very good at something

Tenacious: works hard all the way to the end

Truthful: tells the truth, does not lie, others can believe them

Unique: different, not like any others, one of kind

Useful: offers something others need

Vibrant: bright and colorful, beaming with energy

Valuable: worth a lot to others, matters to others

Wacky: fun in a crazy way

Wild: not boring, out of the ordinary

Whimsical: playful and childlike

Experienced: has had a lot of practice

Extraordinary: so great it is hard to believe

Excellent: very good

Youthful: feeling young and full of life

Yearning: wanting to learn and be better

Zestful: someone who enjoys life

Zany: funny in an odd way

QUESTIONS, EXERCISES AND CHALLENGES

WHAT IS AN AFFIRMATION?

An affirmation is something good you can say about yourself. When you do this and believe what you are saying, it will make you feel good about yourself and will help you to be the person you want to be.

HOW DO YOU USE AFFIRMATIONS?

It's easy. All you have to do is..... say it, believe it and be it. Try the exercises and challenges below to practice.

EXERCISE ONE: Make a list of positive words that best describe you. You may use ones from the book or ones you think of yourself. Write down as many as you can.

EXERCISE TWO: Think about what you would like to be when you grow up and why? Draw a picture of yourself as that.

EXERCISE THREE: Hang the list of words along with your drawing in a place you, your family and/or friends can see it. This will help remind you of how great you are now and of what is possible in the future.

CHALLENGE ONE: Use only positive words to describe yourself for an entire day

BONUS: Use only positive words to describe yourself AND others for a whole WEEK.

CHALLENGE TWO: Each morning for one week choose one word to help yourself through the day. This will be your daily affirmation. Say "Today I am… "

For example: "Today I am brave." "Today I am grateful." "Today I am helpful."

Be sure to repeat the affirmation throughout the day.

BONUS: Each morning for one MONTH choose one word to help yourself through the day.

CPSIA information can be obtained
at www.ICGtesting.com
Printed in the USA
LVHW070614280720
661674LV00003B/48